35 Must-Have Assessment and Record-Keeping Forms for Reading

By Laura Robb

SCHOLASTIC
PROFESSIONAL BOOKS

NEW YORK • TORONTO • LONDON • AUCKLAND • SYDNEY
MEXICO CITY • NEW DELHI • HONG KONG

Dedication

For Bobby and Jaime, with love

Acknowledgments

It's taken many years to collect feedback, then continually adjust and refine the assessment forms in this book. My goal has always been to create forms that teachers and young adolescents will find useful and easy to complete. My sincere and deep thanks to all the students and teachers who, over many years, have shaped the contents of this book. I am especially grateful to teachers I coach at Powhatan School in Boyce, Virginia, and to teachers I mentor and team teach with at Winchester City Schools, at Keister Elementary School in Harrisonburg, Virginia, and at Warren County Junior High in Front Royal, Virginia.

Special thanks go to Terry Cooper, Editor-in-Chief of Scholastic Professional Books, and my editor, Wendy Murray, who came up with the idea of gathering my assessment forms into a book for teachers to adapt and use. The support and confidence in my writing and teaching shown by these two brilliant editors, and their enthusiastic commitment to this project, provided the inspiration that helped me craft a book to help teachers and students become deeply involved in performance-based assessment.

—Laura Robb

Cover design by George Myer and Norma Ortiz
Interior design by LDL Designs
Photographs by Bonnie Forstrum Jacobs

ISBN 0-439-24121-9

Table of Contents

Part 1
What You Need to Know About Assessment and Evaluation

"The district requires us to fill out all these forms on students' reading," a fifth-grade teacher told me. "I fill them out and file them away," she continued, "because there are too many for me to think about, and I don't know what to do with all this information." Too often schools mandate an overwhelming amount of record-keeping without providing the training that enables teachers to actually use these records to help them plan their teaching and improve their students' reading ability. Because it's required, forms are dutifully filled out, yet the process is a waste of teachers' efforts and time because the valuable information collected sits unused. For change in student reading performance to occur, it's necessary to move beyond merely completing reading assessments to interpreting the data and creating teaching plans that address the needs of individual readers.

This book is designed to help teachers make the leap from gathering information to using it to inform their daily teaching. In the following pages you'll find record-keeping and assessment forms that are easy to use and helpful in planning reading instruction. I invite you to select forms you feel will help you in your teaching of reading. The forms include checklists, questionnaires, and note-taking sheets; you can use these in conjunction with standardized tests to construct a comprehensive picture of each student's strengths, needs, and progress. From there, you can formulate teaching plans to help individual readers work on precisely the skills they need to become more fluent readers.

I see these forms as tools of my trade, and they are of no use if they lie dormant in my file cabinet. To make the most of the information I gather, I take time to review forms periodically. Here are some of the ways I use these assessments to support my teaching of reading:

Reread: I review the forms and the observational notes stored in students' folders periodically. Rereading gives me a broader perspective on a reader's needs, since I can see data gathered over several weeks.

Take Notes: While rereading, I jot down notes that highlight what each student does well. I then select two to three areas of need I feel a student can address at that point in the year.

Reflect: I think about my notes and select one strategy or problem the student can improve. I might also decide to bring two or three areas that need work to the student's attention and talk with him or her about which one to address first.

Interpret: I try to figure out what the record-keeping forms and observational notes mean. Often, posing questions such as, *Is this a vocabulary or a prior knowledge problem?* or *Is he or she skimming to find specific details?* helps me work through data.

Evaluate: I create a list of possible interventions, which can range from offering positive feedback to planning targeted mini-lessons to scheduling one-on-one conferences.

Once I reflect on my notes and assessments, I determine what help a student needs from me and plan the best way to deliver that help. I sift through all the options before settling on the most appropriate action. The chart on pages 15–20 offers ideas for you to consider as you reflect on the information you gather about your students from the forms in this book. By adapting these ideas to your students' needs, you'll support their growth in reading.

Keeping Track of Assessment and Record-Keeping Forms

For assessment and evaluation to work, teachers need to collect a variety of data and store the information in a way that's accessible for reflection and for conferences with students, parents, and administrators. The method I prefer is maintaining individual literacy folders for each student.

LITERACY FOLDERS

A literacy folder contains key assessments such as interest and reading surveys and conference and observational notes. These assessments, collected continually throughout the year, inform you about a student's reading strengths and needs, and create a picture of that student's reading growth. By placing data about a student in one file, you can reflect on a variety of assessments taken over time and better understand the kinds of support the student needs.

Finding an accessible place to store the information makes using it less frustrating. Years ago, I would toss all my assessments in a plastic crate, thinking that I'd file them when I had more time. That moment never seemed to arrive, and I'd find myself plowing through piles of papers to sort out the forms for one or two students. Now, I organize file folders in August, before students arrive. Each student has his or her own literacy folder which I store, in alphabetical order, in my filing cabinet. As I a collect or complete assessments, I file the papers that day and try not to procrastinate. The larger the stack becomes, the more daunting the task—and the greater the likelihood of not filing data at all.

What Goes Into a Literacy Folder

Any information that deepens your knowledge of a student's reading process belongs in his or her literacy folder. Detailed record keeping saves me from the impossible task of accurately remembering an event or idea weeks or months later. In addition to surveys and forms that enable me to get to know students throughout the year, I add dated, observational notes; records of reading conferences; error analyses of oral reading (see *Teaching Reading in Middle School,* Scholastic, 2000); and sample journal entries.

I review the folders of struggling readers every other week. I check the folders of other students every four to six weeks. I frequently refer to students' literacy folders to group students with common needs, to help students select appropriate books, to design teaching plans, and to discuss specific reading problems with an administrator, a parent, or a student. Here's what an eighth grader's literacy folder contained in June:

- Standardized test results in Reading and Vocabulary
- Parent/Guardian Information Sheet (see page 24)
- Reading Survey (see page 28)
- What's Easy? What's Hard? (see page 31)
- Reading Strategy Interview (see page 35)
- Getting-to-Know-You Conference (see page 39)
- Observational notes
- Three Reading Strategy Checklists (see pages 47, 48, and 49)
- Two Oral Reading Conference Checklists (see page 59)
- Three journal entries
- Three student self-evaluations (see forms in Part 4)

See samples on page 20 and throughout the book to get a sense of what kinds of information these forms can help you collect.

Note that I did not use every form included in this book. Using too many forms is problematic because you devote your time to collecting record sheets instead of rereading and reflecting on them.

I've designed the checklists and forms in this book to help teachers implement the reading strategy curriculum. While a full description of a reading strategy curriculum is beyond the scope of this book, at its core is the belief that all readers, young and old, use the same strategies to solve reading problems and make meaning from texts (Clay, 1979; Fountas and Pinell, 1996). An overview of the strategic reading approach that these forms support follows. For a more detailed discussion, see *Teaching Reading in Middle School* (Scholastic, 2000).

A Reading Strategy Curriculum

A reading strategy curriculum—also known as a reading comprehension curriculum—is structured around seven strategies that thoughtful readers use to construct meaning and new understandings (Pearson, et al., 1992). I have added two additional strategies—vocabulary-building and fluency—to the seven, for a total of nine. A description of the nine strategies that all readers use to solve print and meaning problems follows.

1. **Activate Prior Knowledge:** The research of schema theorists like Marvin Minsky (1975) and Richard Anderson (1984) demonstrated the relationship between prior knowledge and experience and the comprehension of texts. According to schema theory, each learner brings a unique set of experiences and knowledge, called schemata, to reading. For example, as we read, we use our schemata for weddings to understand marriage ceremonies in Japan, India, or Uganda.

   The research presented by schema theorists informs teachers that getting-ready-to-read strategies have two purposes: 1) Teachers can determine if students have enough background knowledge to read a book or study a topic; and 2) If students' background knowledge is limited, then teachers can enlarge background knowledge before reading to help students improve their comprehension and recall.

2. **Decide What's Important in a Text:** Good readers set purposes before reading and use their goals and prior knowledge to separate unimportant information from key points.

3. **Synthesize Information:** Good readers monitor their comprehension by silently summarizing key points related to their purposes. To do this, readers must set aside irrelevant and repeated information as well as search for topic sentences within the text. If no topic sentence exists, then proficient readers create their own summary sentences.

4. **Draw Inferences During and After Reading:** Good readers read between the lines, searching for unstated, implied meanings based on characters' words, actions,

interaction, and conflicts.

5. **Self-Monitor Comprehension:** Good readers readily identify a confusing or tough passage or an unfamiliar word. Instead of skipping over the challenging text, which is what a struggling reader often does, good readers use fix-it strategies to work through the tricky part of a passage and extract its meaning.

6. **Repair Faulty Comprehension:** Good readers have developed a wide range of fix-it strategies, such as rereading and using context clues, that enable them to understand difficult passages.

7. **Ask Questions:** Posing questions before, during, and after reading is a characteristic of good readers. Questions can set purposes for reading and deepen learners' involvement in the text.

8. **Build Vocabulary:** A poor vocabulary is often the cause of diminished comprehension among middle school students (Barr, Sadow, Blachowicz, 1990). Preteaching and post teaching challenging and new vocabulary, as well as studying prefixes, suffixes, and Greek and Latin roots, can build students' word knowledge.

9. **Read Fluently:** Students who read in a halting, word-by-word manner struggle with phrasing and reading in meaningful chunks. Disfluent readers focus so intensely on pronouncing individual words that they often miss meaning and comprehend and recall little. Teachers can improve fluency by offering students books at their comfort level, by encouraging repeated readings, by having students tape stories for a primary classroom's listening center, and by inviting students to practice reading poetry or a Readers' Theater part with drama and emotion.

WHEN IT COMES TO READING, SHOW, DON'T TELL

In an effective comprehension curriculum, teachers model and demonstrate how reading strategies work in mini-lessons (Atwell, 1987; Calkins, 1986) and think-alouds (Lytle, 1982). **Mini-lessons:** During a mini-lesson, the teacher or a student who is proficient with a strategy demonstrates how he or she uses a reading strategy to either the whole class or a selected small group. In addition to describing the process and showing how the strategy works with a text, the teacher or student also explains how the strategy supports and improves reading comprehension and recall. This demonstration makes visible the in-the-head problem-solving tools readers use to comprehend texts.

These kinds of mini-lessons take from fifteen to twenty-five minutes. Be sure to reserve time for the class to pose questions and to share how they apply the strategy.

Recording a mini-lesson on chart paper facilitates review and reteaching of a concept or strategy. I use a large sheet of chart paper, print the date and the name of the reading strategy at the top of the chart, and hang it on a classroom wall or bulletin board so students can refer to it as they practice a strategy. I then clip completed charts to skirt hangers and store them in a closet or on a hook, making them easily accessible for students who require scaffolding, or more teacher support, before they can apply a strategy independently.

During mini-lessons, you'll isolate a strategy so students can understand and practice it. Once a student understands a strategy, he incorporates it into his repertoire and integrates it with other strategies as he reads to comprehend and construct new knowledge. This means that when a student predicts, for example, he or she is also posing questions, using prior knowledge from the text, making personal connections, and confirming or adjusting predictions.

Think-alouds: A crucial aspect of the mini-lesson, the think-aloud makes public all the questions and anxieties the presenter experiences when applying a strategy (Lytle,1982; Baumann, et al.,1993). Through the think-aloud, teachers and students make visible every thought and reveal how the strategy works for them. As teachers repeatedly model think-alouds and discuss the process, students can learn how to effectively use this strategy. Think-alouds are also very effective in one-on-one conferences.

PLACING READING STRATEGIES IN A THREE-PART READING MODEL

To help you develop students' understanding and application of reading strategies, I've subdivided the core nine presented earlier and organized them into a three-part model (see page 11). Observing how students apply strategies before, during, and after reading helps you assess their strengths and needs as readers. The forms in this book offer a variety of ways for you to step inside a student's mind and better understand his use of reading strategies.

By observing students, conferring with them, inviting them to self-evaluate, and keeping records, you will be able to pinpoint students who can use a strategy independently and those who require more help.

Instructional Scaffolding in a Strategy Curriculum

Struggling middle school readers—those reading more than one year below grade level—can build their vocabulary and improve their comprehension with instructional scaffolding. *Scaffolding* (Graves and Graves, 1994) refers to the specific, individualized support teachers offer students before, during, and after reading. Through your assessment, determine how much support a student needs and provide it through mini-lessons, one-on-

Strategies to Use Before, During, and After Reading

Some Strategies to Use Before Reading	Some Strategies to Use During Reading	Some Strategies to Use After Reading
These activate past knowledge and experiences and let you know if students have enough prior knowledge to comprehend the material.	These enable students to make personal connections, visualize, identify parts that confuse, monitor understanding, and recall information.	These enlarge past knowledge and can create connections to other texts.

• Brainstorm/Categorize	• Make Personal Connections	• Skim
• Predict/Support	• Use Prior Knowledge	• Reread
• Skim/Preview	• Predict/Support/ Adjust or Confirm	• Question
• Pose Questions	• Pose Questions	• Visualize
• Fast-Write	• Identify Confusing Parts	• Evaluate and Adjust Predictions
• Preteach Vocabulary	• Visualize	• Reflect Through Talking, Writing, Drawing
• What Do I Know? What's New?	• Self-Monitor for Understanding	• Infer; Compare/Contrast; Cause/Effect; Concluding; Thesis/Proof
• Visualize/Recall Other Sensory Experiences	• Summarize	• Take Notes
	• Synthesize	• Summarize
	• Reread	• Synthesize
	• Use Context Clues	
	• Infer	

one conferences, or by pairing the student with a peer. All of these interactions focus on helping the student apply a particular strategy, such as predict/support or selecting important details. Gradually reduce the amount of scaffolding as the student gains confidence. The goal is complete independence in applying the strategy.

The three-part reading model (Dowhower, 1999; Robb, 1995, 2000) suggests a framework for scaffolding possibilities that can move all readers forward—whether struggling or proficient.

As you plan your reading sessions, think of your readers, their needs, and the kinds of

Scaffolding Suggestions in the Three-Part Reading Framework

The following teaching ideas can help you provide the support your students need to learn and use various reading strategies. Depending on your students' needs, you can model or think-aloud about reading strategies in a variety of settings—from a whole-class mini-lesson to a one-on-one conference. These strategies can improve students' comprehension, recall of important details, and ability to link what they know to new information.

Teaching Strategies That Support Students Before Reading	Teaching Strategies That Support Students During Reading	Teaching Strategies That Support Students After Reading
• Activate prior knowledge	• Set purposes	• Raise questions
• Build background knowledge	• Self-monitor what's understood and what's confusing	• Discuss
• Connect the book or topic to students' lives	• Reread	• Write
• Preteach vocabulary	• Figure out a word's meaning from context clues	• Dramatize
• Preteach new concepts	• Pose questions	• Draw
• Predict	• Predict/Support/Confirm/Adjust	• Reteach
• Raise questions	• Visualize	• Confer
• Set purposes for reading	• Read and retell	
• Be explicit about the reading strategy you will practice	• Guided practice with teacher	
	• Read passages aloud to student	
	• Tape passages	
	• Find alternate texts that the student can read	

opportunities that would help them progress. Use the list of teaching ideas on page 12 as a starting point for whole-class, small-group, and individual reading experiences. Keep in mind, however, that there are some experiences that should always be part of your instructional plan; an overview of these follows.

Before Reading:

1. Always activate and assess students' prior knowledge, and decide whether to plunge into the study or reserve time to build prior knowledge through read alouds, picture books, filmstrips, a field trip, or presentations by knowledgeable people.

2. Name the strategy students will be practicing, model how it works, and point out ways the strategy can benefit a reader (Dowhower, 1999). Students will access and apply strategies they know and have practiced; naming a strategy gives you and students a common vocabulary to talk about reading.

During Reading:

Set purposes for reading. Having specific purposes enables students to separate important information from nonessential ideas (Keene and Zimmermann, 1998), and learners are more likely to engage with a text when they have real and meaningful reasons to read.

After Reading:

Talk about the text. Talk clarifies what students understand, helps them connect information to what they know, broadens their knowledge base as they exchange ideas with peers, and enables them to construct new understandings (Alvermann, 1998; Gambrell, 1999).

Always include the above components and, depending on time and students' needs, add other scaffolding experiences to support their progress in reading. For those students reading two or more years below grade level, the scaffolding ideas listed on pages 15–20 work well within the context of the reading strategy curriculum that Pearson, et al. (1992) and Robb (2000) discuss.

SCAFFOLDING FOR STRUGGLING READERS

For some students, one whole-class mini-lesson followed by one or two group mini-lessons and in-class practice is not enough. To absorb a strategy, these students need one-on-one sessions with their teacher. The chart that begins on page 15 lists reading strategies and scaffolding suggestions you can try with students. In addition, I've included some student behaviors that indicate the need for extra support. Usually students exhibit

several of these behaviors. If a student generates few ideas in brainstorming, finds the
material boring, and fails to ask questions, you may conclude that he or she is not
employing the strategy of activating prior knowledge and can plan your intervention
accordingly. Sometimes it's difficult to sort through all the behaviors you see, but the
more experience you gain observing students, the better equipped you'll be to decide
which strategies to scaffold. Recording your observations on the forms in this book and
then reflecting on them are the first steps toward knowing how to best support a student.

Asking a student what strategies he needs help with is also effective. A fifth grader
told his teacher, "I know about the Middle Ages. I can't read it [the book] 'cause words
are too hard. Can't say them. Don't know what they mean." Once made aware of the
problem, the teacher was able to find an alternate book on the Middle Ages that the student could read.

As you scaffold students' reading, you'll adapt suggestions to students' specific needs.
If a student does not respond to one support framework, try another. Always take the
time to ask a student why she thinks a fix-it strategy isn't helping. This information can
help you evaluate your intervention plan. Follow these suggestions:

- Start by modeling the strategy for the student.
- Invite the student to raise questions.
- Respond to the queries.
- Have the student practice the strategy under your guidance. At first, share the work—
  you read and think-aloud, then the student takes a turn.
- Use small sections of text. Start with one to two sentences, then increase the amount
  slowly. Your observations and interactions will enable you to decide how much of the
  process to turn over to the student.
- Continue practicing with the student until she can work independently. You can also
  use a competent peer tutor to support the student.
- Select the instructional scaffolding that you believe will best benefit the student.

The chart on pages 15-20 will help you observe your students' reading behaviors so
you can target which strategy to work on next. In addition to identifying their strengths
and needs, it's helpful to start learning about your students' interests and reading lives as
soon as school opens. The more you know about their attitudes, outside interests, and
strengths, the better equipped you'll be to find the books and materials that will best
support their progress. Part 2 provides a variety of forms that help you collect this kind
of information.

Teaching Reading Strategies

STRATEGY	SCAFFOLDING	STUDENT BEHAVIOR
Activate Prior Knowledge	• Build background knowledge with pictures, read alouds, filmstrips, talk, and field trips. • Use book title, chapter titles, boldface headings, pictures, charts, graphs, and captions to increase prior knowledge. • Work one-on-one to use prior knowledge from a text to predict and/or answer questions. • Think aloud and show how you use prior knowledge to predict/support/confirm/adjust and/or answer questions. • Discuss ways to collect background knowledge from other students and teachers. • Map what you know and add to the map as you learn more. • Preteach key vocabulary. • Preteach key concepts.	• Offers few ideas in brain-storming. • Teacher observation of pre-reading experience notes poor prior knowledge. • Finds material boring. • Doesn't pose questions. • Has no ideas under the "Know" of a KWL (Know, Want to Know, Learn) • Doesn't participate in pre-reading experiences. • Displays poor recall after reading. • Doesn't predict. • Doesn't make personal connections.
Decide What's Important	• Do a one-on-one think-aloud, then take turns with the student. • Set purposes and select details that relate to the purposes. • Preview titles, section headings, pictures and captions, graphs and charts in a textbook. • Use boldface words for clues. • In a novel, study the title,	• Unable to select important details. • Doesn't set reading purposes. • Avoids previewing. • Doesn't skim and reread. • Doesn't know how to skim. • Sees no purpose in skimming. • Doesn't make personal connections.

STRATEGY	SCAFFOLDING	STUDENT BEHAVIOR
Decide What's Important (cont.)	cover, illustrations, and chapter titles. • Note important details on sticky notes. • After reading, skim and create a web. • Discuss and help student connect what's important to his or her life.	• Has difficulty with webbing, mapping. • Has difficulty with note-taking. • Resists taking notes. • Says the text is too difficult to read. • Has little prior knowledge.
Synthesize	• Read/Pause/Retell • Demonstrate how you select details that relate to the purpose for reading. • Think about purpose for reading and select key details. • Think aloud and show how you use details to create your own main idea. • Paired questioning: Take turns asking questions about short sections that help the reader focus on key points. • Paired summarizing: Take turns summarizing short passages.	• Retells instead of summarizing. • Has difficulty selecting key events, ideas. • Struggles to generalize main ideas from details. • Doesn't set purposes. • Says the text is too difficult to read. • Has little prior knowledge.
Infer	• Help student understand that an inference is an implied or unstated idea. • Model how you infer what a character thinks and/or feels from dialogue, interactions with others, inner thoughts, conflicts, settings. • Study text structure and look at clues author leaves when telling how a character spoke, acted, looked.	• Looks for literal meanings. • Has difficulty connecting to characters. • Doesn't study character's thoughts, actions. • Doesn't create mental and sensory images. • Has difficulty using details to discover themes. • Has little prior knowledge.

STRATEGY	SCAFFOLDING	STUDENT BEHAVIOR
Infer (cont.)	• Study author tags in dialogue, such as "shouted," "wept," "muttered." • Show how you infer what a character thinks and feels or why a decision was made by connecting the character's experiences to your own. • Model how you imagine a character's tone of voice and inner thoughts to help you make inferences. • Help student visualize a character's expressions and gestures and decide what can be inferred from these. • Help students understand the meaning of themes: large general ideas that a book explores through characters, plot, and settings. • Show students how you take specific details from a text to develop thematic statements.	
Self-Monitor	• Place tough words on sticky notes, with page number and title of book. • Help students use context clues in the text or to figure out meanings. • Explain why it's important to identify confusing passages. • Show how to access fix-it strategies, such as rereading. • Read and summarize sections to see if you recall details.	• Skips confusing passages, new words. • Doesn't pause to figure out new words. • Doesn't self-check; fails to summarize while reading to monitor comprehension. • Recall lacks details. • Does not connect material to prior knowledge. • Has little prior knowledge.

STRATEGY	SCAFFOLDING	STUDENT BEHAVIOR
Ask Questions	• Model how questions prior to reading help set clear purposes for reading a text. • Show how texts don't answer all questions. • Model how questions posed while reading keep you engaged with the text and help make personal connections and access prior knowledge. • Use a sticky note to model pausing and posing questions with short passages. • Show how to raise post-reading questions for discussions. Let student know that talking about a book clarifies ideas, helps recall of details, and enables readers to connect to self, other books, and local and world issues.	• Does not pose questions before or during reading. • Says the text is too difficult to read. • Uninterested in content of text. • Does not make personal connections. • Does not connect material to prior knowledge.
Skim	• Show how you use information in a question, or a key word or phrase, to help you skim a narrative text. • Show how you try to recall where you think you'll find the information: the beginning, middle, or end of a chapter, story, or book. • Use captions, pictures, charts, graphs, headings, and/or bold-face words to think aloud, showing how each element helps you locate information. • Model how you reread small sections once you've skimmed and located the passage, explaining how the skimming and rereading support recall.	• Can't determine what sections to skim. • Rereads everything instead of skimming. • Says the text is too difficult to read. • Lacks prior knowledge. • Has poor recall of where information is in the text. • Says that skimming is a waste of time.

STRATEGY	SCAFFOLDING	STUDENT BEHAVIOR
Predict/ Support	• Model using prior knowledge to make logical predictions • Confirm/Adjust predictions. • Show how you skim to find details that support predictions. • Make sure students can read the text. • Field student questions about the strategy. • Help students redo their predictions. • Model the difference between support that's too general and detailed examples from the text.	• Predictions are not logical. • Support does not come from the text. • Does not adjust predictions. • Wants to always be right. • Doesn't predict. • Says the text is too difficult to read. • Doesn't make personal connections. • Lacks prior knowledge.
Build Vocabulary	• Preteach important words. • Preteach key concepts. • Create antonym and synonym webs. • Build words from Greek and Latin roots and demonstrate how a knowledge of the meaning of a root can help you understand an unfamiliar word. • Teach prefixes and suffixes and how these help you figure out a word's meaning. • Show how to use the dictionary to find the definition of a word that connects to the author's use of the word.	• Lacks knowledge of the book's concepts. • Has poor knowledge of roots, prefixes, suffixes. • Lacks strategies for figuring out words in context. • Doesn't connect new words or concepts to prior knowledge. • Has poor dictionary skills.
Read Fluently	• Demonstrate repeated readings. • Use poems with strong rhythm and rhyme for repeated readings.	• Reads with many stops and hesitations. • Struggles to "sound out" many words.

STRATEGY	SCAFFOLDING	STUDENT BEHAVIOR
Read Fluently (cont.)	• Read a phrase or sentence with expression and rhythm and ask the student to imitate you. Continue practicing with short passages until student achieves fluency. • Have students gain fluency by reading easy books, then tape record stories for listening centers in primary grades. • Organize reading buddies so that disfluent readers practice reading easy books with fluency, then read to younger students.	• Has limited comprehension due to word-to-word reading. • Avoids oral reading to support a point. • Texts are too difficult to read.

Checklists and anecdotal notes like these excerpted from an eight grader's literacy folder help you record behaviors so you can consider what scaffolding would be most appropriate for a student.

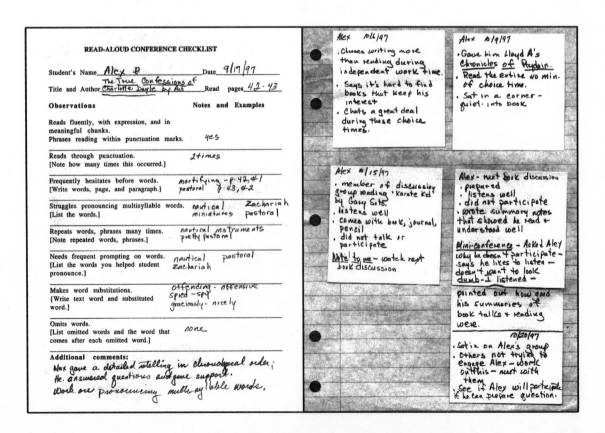

Part 2

Getting to Know Your Students as Readers

I started my first two years of teaching by immediately plunging into the curriculum. My colleagues did the same. Getting to know the students in our classes occurred as weeks and months passed, almost incidentally, as we focused on covering the curriculum. Not until November or December did we have a solid grasp of the kind of support our twenty-five to thirty students needed. Today, as I reflect on those beginning teaching years, I know that too much time elapsed before I gained insights into the strengths and needs of each student.

I quickly recognized the benefits of collecting as much information as possible about each student before school opened and during the first month. My quest for information now begins in August, when I review the standardized test results of students, confer with last year's teacher, and review the contents of the portfolios that have been delivered to my classroom. Reading students' writing samples and self-evaluations of their progress provides additional insights.

Not all schools maintain reading/writing portfolios, and students new to our school don't have these. But using the information I have available, I create two lists:

1. Names of students reading one or more years below grade level.

2. Names of students reading at or above grade level.

These tentative lists enable me to organize teacher-led strategic reading groups (see *Teaching Reading in Middle School),* pair students for book discussions, and focus on meeting first with readers who struggle, so I can plan interventions as soon as possible. As I collect information from parents, student survey forms, and one-on-one interviews and conferences, I adjust these lists.

In this section, you will find a variety of assessment forms that enable you to better know students by the time the first month of school has ended. *Choose those that you feel are appropriate for your teaching situation.*

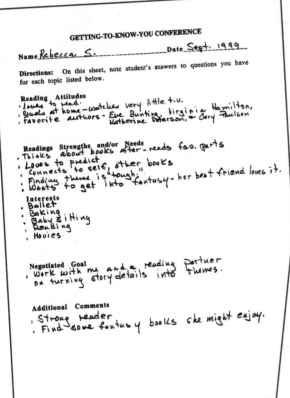

Getting-to-Know-You Conference forms help me gauge students' attitudes about reading and give me insight into the kinds of support that will work best for them.

Parent/Guardian Information Sheet

PURPOSE:
To collect vital information about students from parents' perspectives; to open communication and establish school/home connections.

A student's performance and behavior at school reveals only one aspect of that child. To broaden our knowledge of the students we teach, it's important to learn about their out-of-school lives. That's why I start the year by collecting information from their parents or caretakers. Inviting adults to share what they know about their children honors them, opens lines of communication, and can provide teachers with valuable information about students' study habits, interests, and attitudes toward school. Moreover, the Information Sheet also lets me know the level of involvement with school that each family can manage.

Research completed for CIERA (Center for the Improvement of Early Reading Achievement) by Barbara M. Taylor, et al., showed that a primary indicator of the most effective schools was having strong links to parents. I have found that strengthening the links between families and middle schools often translates into more home support for young adolescent readers.

Students take these sheets home the first day of school with a cover letter (see page 25) that asks parents to return them by the end of the week. By the end of the third or fourth week of school when I make my first telephone call home, I use the responses to open positive conversations.

You can preplan and document important telephone and in-person conferences with parents using the form on page 26.

Parent/Guardian Information Sheet

Student's Name _____ Date _____

Teacher _____

1 Please list your child's strong points as a reader and a learner:

2 List your child's interests and hobbies:

3 List what you and your child enjoy doing together:

4 Offer any tips or suggestions that might help me help your child learn:

5 If you have time, list some ways you would like to be involved with your child's education:

WHEN IS THE BEST TIME TO CALL YOU? _____

Cover Letter to Parents
That You Can Adapt

August 2000

Dear Mrs. Delaney,

Because I value what you know about your son, Justin, I am asking you to complete the enclosed Information Sheet. Please take the entire week to think about these questions, respond to them, and return the sheet on Friday.

Sharing the knowledge you have about Justin will provide me with important information, enabling me to support his reading and writing during his eighth grade year. Besides the observations you share, Justin and his classmates will complete surveys and interviews that will give me additional information. I will use all of this data to guide Justin's reading, help him find books he can't put down, and improve his writing and speaking.

During the last week of September, I will telephone you to discuss your observations and any questions you may have. Should you want to speak to me sooner, please call in the evening.

Sincerely,

Laura Robb

Parent-Teacher Conference Form

Student's Name _____ Date _____

Names of Adults Who Participated:

Topics the Teacher Wishes to Discuss:

Issues, Questions, Concerns Parents Raised:

Recommendations and Goals:

Additional Teacher Comments:

Reading and Interest Surveys

PURPOSE:
To learn about students' interests and attitudes towards reading so you can help them select books and gain insights into the kinds of support they might need.

Before asking students to complete one or both of these surveys (see pages 28 and 29), reserve time to show students how you answer the questions. By thinking aloud you give students a glimpse of your reading life and how you spend your spare time. At the same time, you provide them with a model of how you answer the questions on the surveys. In addition, reserve time to discuss why it's important for responses to contain specific details and how this information is helpful. Encourage students to ask questions. Set aside time for them to discuss survey prompts with a partner, for talk reclaims prior experiences and can stimulate memory. Here's my introduction:

When you tell me about your interests, favorite books, and the strategies that you apply before and during reading, you're helping me get to know you and supplying valuable information that I can use to help you. These surveys enable me to suggest titles I think you'll enjoy and explore ways I can help you improve your reading. I'll also find those of you with common interests—people who might enjoy reading and discussing the same book or working on a project together.

You'll find there is a relationship between the preparation and modeling you do and the quality of students' answers. I always invite students to respond in class where they can chat with a partner, use me as a resource, and have enough time to be thoughtful about their answers.

INTEREST SURVEY

Name Vincent C.   Date Sept. 10 '98

Complete each statement.

1. When I have free time I like to roller blade- ride bikes
2. My favorite indoor games are nintendo
3. My favorite outdoor games are hoops - soccer
4. Topics I'd like to learn more about are guitar
5. The music I like best is rap
6. The subject I like best at school is gym because I get to play hoops and be with my buddies
7. The books I choose are usually about sports
8. When I'm with friends we like to hang out - talk
9. Some of my favorite movies are Home Alone and Nutty Prof.
10. The things I enjoy most at school are gym - lunch - a
11. If I could travel somewhere, it would be CA because my grandparents live there.
12. If I had $50.00, I would spend it on tapes, guitar lessons

A sixth grader's completed Interest Survey.

Reading Survey

Name _____ Date _____

Fill in the blanks.

1. What words pop into your mind when you think of reading a book?

   _____

2. Do you read at home?_____ How often do you read at home?_____

3. Where's your favorite place to read at home? _____ At school?_____

4. How do you find books you love to read? _____

5. Besides books, what other types of materials do you read? _____

   _____ Why do you enjoy these?_____

6. Do you own a library card?_____ How often do you visit the library to check

   out books?_____

Complete these sentences.

7. My favorite author is _____

8. The best book I've read is _____

9. The best book someone read to me is _____

10. The topics I enjoy reading about are _____

11. I watch TV for _____ hours a day because _____

12. The things I'm great at as a reader are _____

   _____

13. Things I need to work on to improve my reading are _____

   _____

14. I use these strategies as I read: _____

   _____

15. I enjoy talking about books because _____

16. I enjoy responding to books in discussions because _____

   _____

17. I enjoy responding to books in my journal because _____

   _____

18. I can choose books that I can read for enjoyment because _____

Interest Survey

Name _____ Date _____

Complete each statement.

1. When I have free time I like to _____

2. My favorite indoor games are _____

3. My favorite outdoor games are _____

4. Topics I'd like to learn more about are _____

5. The music I like best is _____

6. The subject I like best at school is _____ because _____

_____

7. The books I choose are usually about _____

8. When I'm with friends we like to _____

9. Some of my favorite movies are _____

10. The things I enjoy most at school are _____

11. If I could travel somewhere, it would be _____ because _____

_____

12. If I had $50.00, I would spend it on _____

The "What's Easy? What's Hard?" Strategy

PURPOSE:

To obtain information that illustrates how students see themselves as readers; to discover, early in the year, students' reading strengths and needs.

Pose the "What's easy/hard?" questions and invite students to reflect on their reading lives. Before asking students to respond on the form, use a think-aloud to model how you organize your answers. Write the prompts on chart paper, then think-aloud to make the process visible. Here's what I think aloud for What's Hard About Reading and Why? and What's Easy About Reading and Why?:

Lots of thoughts bombard my mind. I have to admit that reading can be tough for me, especially when it's on a new topic or about something that doesn't capture my interest, or when it's a boring, fact-packed textbook that has no stories. Having to cope with many unfamiliar words makes reading hard.

Reading mysteries is easy because it's one of my favorite genres. I also find reading about topics I love easy, because I have lots of background knowledge to help me understand. Short action stories in magazines are enjoyable because I can finish them in one sitting. I also find reading education journals and books easy because of my rich prior knowledge and intense interest in these.

Next, jot down notes under each question, modeling that thinking precedes note-taking and writing. Then, invite students to ask questions and discuss your responses. Most students experience relief and express delight to learn that I encounter tough reading situations. "It helps me to know that you have trouble with some books," a seventh grader said. For those who say, "I don't know" or "I have nothing to say," ask them to write those words on the paper. In a conference, you can explore reasons why a student can't write about his or her reading process.

What's Easy? What's Hard?

Name _____ Date _____

What's Easy About Reading? Why?

What's Hard About Reading? Why?

Eleven Questions About Reading

PURPOSE:
To discover how students see themselves as readers; to discover what students know about the writing process.

The eleven questions on page 33 are a terrific way to start modeling aspects of the writing process for your students as well as to collect valuable information about their reading lives. Meanwhile, this is the ideal time to share information about yourself as a reader. My son, Evan, a teacher who struggled with reading when he was in the primary grades, annually told his sixth graders, "Learning to read was tough for me. I was a slow reader and had trouble pronouncing long words. But once I learned and practiced some strategies, and found books I could read, I started to improve." It's helpful to share your struggles or the struggles of someone you know with students, so they realize that they aren't the only ones who have experienced reading frustration.

During three separate workshops, I model on chart paper how to take notes for the questions. For three questions, I transform the notes into a paragraph, then invite students to ask questions and discuss the process. It takes fifteen to twenty minutes of three to four workshops for students to complete their note-taking and writing. All this time, I circulate among students, for I want to be available to answer questions, listen to them talk through ideas, and offer as much support as possible.

Reading can make me feel sick sometimes because if I read for a long period of time I I will get sick. I don't like to read unless I like the book. Things I think of whenever I read is what if I want to read more of or just quit the book. What I do well as a reader is knowing whos speaking. I read any place it is quite and not noisy. My faivrit Authors is R.L. Stine I don't like any other Authors I like mystry books

A fifth grader composed this response after brainstorming answers for Eleven Questions About Reading.

Eleven Questions About Reading

Directions: Read the questions that follow. On separate paper, take notes for each question. For each question, write up your notes in a paragraph. If you can't answer a question, write "I don't know."

1. Why do you read?

2. What benefits do you see in reading? How do you think reading helps you in your daily life?

3. What do you do well as a reader?

4. Do you read for pleasure at home? How often? What do you enjoy reading?

5. How does reading make you feel?

6. How do you select a book to read for enjoyment?

7. What do you do with the book before you start reading it?

8. As you read, are you aware of any strategies you use when you don't understand a word? A passage?

9. When you finish a book, what do you do?

10. What are some of your favorite books?

11. Do you have a favorite author? Why do you enjoy this author's book?

Reading Strategy Interview Form

PURPOSE:

To discover what students know about reading strategies; to learn what strategies they use before, while, and after reading.

This survey is especially helpful for fifth- and sixth-grade middle-school teachers who know little about their students because it is the students' first year in middle school. I also conduct these interviews with students new to our district to deepen my knowledge of the strategies they know and use.

Always inform students that as they talk, you'll jot down notes so you can accurately recall their words. This way you'll avoid students thinking that you are recording "bad" things about them. Invite students to read your notes at the end of the interview; I find that often, rereading or hearing me reread the notes jogs students' memories and they offer additional information.

Immediately, you gather information that enables you to decide which students to group and which to offer one-on-one support. Responses such as "I know I should reread hard parts, but I don't," or "I try to pick a book on a topic I enjoy and the pages look easy enough to me," or "At times I think about a character I liked after I finish," reveal some experience with strategic reading. Organize these students into small groups and build on their knowledge and experience.

Students who have no strategic reading background will answer, "I don't know" or "Nothing." They will progress faster through short individual meetings where you can attend to their specific needs.

My notes on a Reading Strategy Interview with an eighth grader.

READING STRATEGY INTERVIEW

Directions: On this paper, jot down notes as you converse with a student.

Student's Name **Anthony I.**   Date **Sept. 29, 1999**

1a. How do you choose a book?
- Friend tells me, "You gotta read this."
- Teacher recommends
- Book cover

1b. How do you know that you can read and enjoy the book?
- I try a few pages. That helps me know if I'll like it.

2. What do you do with the book before you start reading?
- Look at title, picture on cover, read back. Think—What do I know abt. this stuff.

3. While reading, what do you do if you bump into a word or section that you don't understand?
- I reread. I try to find clues in the sentences. If I can't get it—I go on.

4. How do you help yourself remember the details of your reading?
- I think about what I read. If I don't remember much—I reread. I predict and ask questions—looking for answers helps me remember.

5. When you complete a book, what do you do?
- Think about my favorite character. Reread parts that were cool. Tell a friend if it was good.

Strengths: lots of strategies: prior knowledge, predict, question, reread, context clues, reflects, recommends books. reading is important.

One or Two Goals Negotiated with Student:
① Introduce and practice writing tough words, page on — with a Post-it.
② 5 finger method to see if the book is at independent level.

Reading Strategy Interview

Student's Name _____ Date _____

Directions: On this paper, jot down notes as you converse with a student.

1a. How do you choose a book?

1b. How do you know that you can read and enjoy the book?

2. What do you do with the book before you start reading?

3. While reading, what do you do if you hit a word or section that you don't understand?

4. How do you help yourself remember the details of your reading?

5. When you complete a book, what do you do?

Strengths:

Reading Strategy Checklist

PURPOSE:
To help students become more aware of their own process and reading habits.

Before asking students to complete this checklist, reserve time to explain the term *strategies* so students understand the meaning of the items. In a think-aloud, I explain the term this way:

> *A strategy is a tool stored in your memory and experience that can help you figure out the meaning of a tough word or select important information from a book. So, if a word or sentence confuses me, I'll reread to see if that helps. If I'm still confused, I'll look for clues in the sentence or paragraph that might help. The more reading strategies I have, the better equipped I am to solve reading problems.*

Explain that you will use this checklist to help students improve their reading. Invite students to fill out this list during the second or third week of school. At this time, the list will offer insights into the type of reading instruction students have had and recall. The first checklist is a baseline against which students can measure their progress as they complete the same form halfway through the year and near the close of the year. It's a simple way for students to monitor and clearly observe their growth in accessing and applying strategies before, while, and after reading.

Reading Strategy Checklists completed by a seventh grader at the beginning and end of the year. She has added several reading strategies to her repertoire during the year.

Reading Strategy Checklist

Name _____ Date _____

BEFORE READING...

____ I think about the cover, title, and what I know about the topic.

____ I skim, looking at and thinking about pictures, photos, graphs, charts.

____ I read headings and captions.

____ I read the back cover and/or print on the inside of the jacket.

____ I use the five finger method to see if the book is just right for me.

____ I ask questions.

____ I make predictions.

WHILE READING...

____ I make mental pictures.

____ I identify confusing parts and reread these.

____ I use pictures, graphs, and charts to understand confusing parts.

____ I identify unfamiliar words and use context clues to figure out their meanings.

____ I stop and retell to see what I remember. If necessary, I reread.

____ I predict and adjust or confirm.

____ I raise questions and read on to discover answers.

____ I jot down a tough word and the page it's on and ask for help.

AFTER READING...

____ I think about the characters, settings, events, or new information.

____ I discuss or write my reactions.

____ I reread parts I enjoy.

____ I skim to find details.

____ I reread to find support for questions.

Getting-to-Know-You Reading Conference Form

PURPOSE:

To use data from students to learn more about their reading process; to open one-on-one communication with students; to set initial reading goals.

Plan on using the weeks from mid-September to the end of October to complete and document an eight- to ten-minute conference with each student. I create two lists of students' names. One has students with low standardized test scores who tell me they hate reading, it's hard, or they don't know what to say, and those who know little to nothing about strategic reading. Those students land on my "See ASAP" list. The remainder of the class goes on my second list; I confer with them next.

To prevent conferences from derailing, here is a planning checklist:

1. Tell students that you will be taking notes during the conference to recall key details and figure out ways to help students improve reading. Invite students to read what you wrote so they don't think you've recorded negative comments.

2. Think of some openers; you'll find these in students' responses that you've collected from surveys and interviews. Here are some you can adapt:
   - Can you tell me why you wrote nothing about yourself?
   - I read that you enjoy sports. Do you belong to a team?
   - You wrote that all reading is hard. Can you tell me something specific that makes it hard for you?
   - You write that you hate to read. What about reading makes you hate it?
   - You wrote that you've never found a book you enjoy. Can you tell me some of your interests or the movies you really enjoy?
   - Is there anything you'd like to tell me that you haven't written about?
   - I see that Betsy Byars is your favorite author. What about her books appeals to you?

3. Invite students to participate in the goal-setting process. Use a prompt instead of a question to move beyond an "I don't know" response. Try, "Tell me what you think you need to work on next." If that doesn't elicit some suggestions, ask the student to reread your notes and offer a suggestion. When there is still no response, I suggest two to three goals and ask the student to select one. It's crucial to negotiate, so students feel part of the process and have a desire to meet the new goal.

Getting-to-Know-You Conference

Name _____ Date _____

Directions: On this sheet, note student's answers to questions you have for each topic listed below.

Reading Attitudes:

Readings Strengths and/or Needs:

Interests:

Negotiated Goal:

Additional Comments:

Part 3

Assessment Forms That Help You Observe Students

As you observe students reading silently, working in groups or with a partner, conferring with you, and as you read their journal entries, you'll collect valuable information. Yetta Goodman (1985) called this observation process "kid-watching" and stated that by systematically watching students, teachers could develop a theory of how each child learns. The purpose of systematic observation is to identify each student's strengths and needs and formulate a plan of support (Routman, 2000).

Observing students can provide you with vital information about each child's reading process and attitudes, information that complements the data from standardized and teacher-made tests, oral reading error analyses (see page 59), interviews, and student work. This range of assessments helps you construct a complete picture of a child's reading ability; your observations are an integral piece of that picture.

Of course, observing and recording student reading behavior is time-consuming. While the forms in this section help make the task manageable, using them effectively requires a commitment of time and effort. Choose one or two forms you think will work well for you, and try them out first, taking time to feel comfortable using them. Then, add any checklists that will help you flesh out your picture of a student as a reader. If you take observational notes on a regular basis, you can attach these to a checklist and evaluate items your notes have not addressed.

The trick is finding a balance between jotting observations on sticky notes and completing checklists. When you feel anxious and overwhelmed, take stock of how much you are doing and lighten your assessment load.

Mastering Observational Note-Taking

If you're a novice at taking observational notes, start small and set aside five to ten minutes twice a week to observe one student at a time. Once you've gained confidence, try observing two and then three students a day as they read and write independently or discuss books, confer, or complete projects in pairs or groups.

TIPS FOR TAKING USEFUL OBSERVATIONAL NOTES

- Use sticky notes. Place the student's name, the date, and the situation at the top of the note (see samples below).
- Carry sticky notes and a pencil all the time.
- Let students know what you are doing so they don't assume you are writing "bad" things about them.
- Jot down notes about a student in different learning situations.
- Use shorthand as you write what you see and hear.
- Do not editorialize.
- Share observations with students. Let them know in a brief conference that what you've observed can help you and them negotiate reasonable goals.
- If you've observed problem behavior, simply state what you saw. Resist an accusatory tone. Then, ask probing questions that encourage the student to solve the problem.
- Store notes on a sheet of paper in students' literacy folders.
- Reread these notes and continually update your literacy plans for students.

Ricardo — 3/14 (Grade 8)
Group Discussion

- didn't bring book, journal
- talked about soccer game
- wrote nothing in journal

Rosanna — 2/23 (Grade 6)
Independent Reading

- draws on paper
- opens book after I ask her to
- turns pages quickly
- talks to Sean
- asks to go to bathroom
- after 10 minutes, reads

BEHAVIORS TO NOTE

The examples that follow can help you become skilled at observing your students. These are a starting point—be as specific as you can in your notes. For example: Questions show mini-lesson did not connect—do small group; silent throughout; watched closely. Always note all behaviors you see. It's just as important to record and share positive behaviors as it is problem ones. These samples are suggestions that can help you become a top-notch observer. Use them to focus on what students do and do not say, how they interact with others, and how they react to independent reading.

During/After Mini-Lessons:

- Listens to demonstration
- Studies chart carefully
- Asks questions
- Shares strategies and process
- Remains silent in follow-up discussion
- Shows confusion during questions/statements

During Sustained Silent Reading (Independent Reading):

- Settles into reading quickly
- Fidgets, moves around for a long time
- Frequently talks to others
- Concentrates on book
- Occasionally pauses to share a section
- Changes books several times

During Book Discussions:

- Comes prepared with book, pencil, journal
- Reads assigned pages
- Listens while others speak
- Participates in discussion
- Takes notes when appropriate
- Values others' ideas
- Supports points with story
- Reads examples from text to prove points
- Shares in group decision-making

Checklists and forms like these help me note behavior when I see it, so I can reflect on it later and use my observations to create targeted teaching plans.

During Short Conferences:

- Talks about issues
- Can/cannot explain confusions
- Participates in goal-setting
- Can apply strategies to reading

After Strategic Reading Group Meets:

- Comes prepared with book, pencil, and journal
- Reads assigned pages
- Shows an understanding of strategy
- Talks about how strategy works
- Understands how strategy helps reading
- Asks probing questions
- Shares process
- Uses text to show an understanding of strategy

During Paired Reading:

- Listens carefully
- Follows text as partner reads
- Retells sections in great detail
- Supports partner
- Skims, rereads to improve retellings

Watching Students Write in Journals:

- Heads page correctly
- Follows journal-entry guidelines
- Returns to book to collect specific details
- Stays on task
- Volunteers to share entry with group/class

Reading Students' Journal Entries:

- Follows guidelines
- Offers support from text
- Uses story details
- Shows understanding of character/setting/plot/theme
- Makes inferences from text

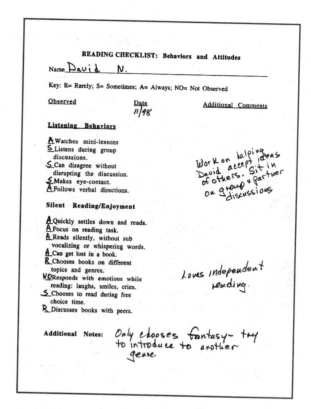

This checklist will remind me to introduce David to other genres and to help him accept others' ideas during literature discussions.

FORMS THAT HELP YOU
OBSERVE STUDENTS

Making Informed Decisions

There's no magic recipe for using collected data to group students or to tell you exactly when and how to intervene with a student. As you read students' records, talk with them, collect information from conferences and writing, and confer with last year's teachers, you will be able to identify students' needs and know where to place them. The key point here is to base your decisions on what you learn about students and know that these decisions will change as students improve.

Watching your students as they work in pairs, groups, or alone, and then reflecting on what you've observed, can also inform your teaching decisions. Think about and complete the checklist that follows. It will provide insights into your observation style.

Student Observation Style Checklist

_____ I circulate around the room and rarely sit at my desk.

_____ I pause and chat briefly with each student to learn about their reading and thinking.

_____ I observe, for five to ten minutes each day, one to two students and jot down objective notes about what I see.

_____ I read students' written responses to literature to learn more about their recall and comprehension.

By watching the students in your classroom, you'll come to understand how they process print. Moreover, as you reread your observational notes and checklists, you'll gain insights into whether or not students can apply a strategy to a variety of reading materials.

How Do I Know That Students Can Use a Strategy?

• Circulate and watch students during guided practice.

• Observe partners practicing a strategy.

• Note how students apply a strategy during guided strategic reading groups.

• Discuss a strategy during one-on-one meetings with students.

• Read students' journal entries and self-evaluations.

Key Reading Strategies

The list that follows will help you to identify some key reading strategies that proficient readers use.

Strategy	Readers Gain Control Over
Select Appropriate Books	Choosing readable books that can support growth in fluency, word knowledge, and comprehension.
Make Connections	Relating their experiences and knowledge to information read in the text.
Visualize	Increasing comprehension when they create mental pictures of information they understand.
Predict/Support	Engaging with the text, setting purposes, and finding evidence that supports predictions.
Confirm/Adjust	Confirming or adjusting predictions while they read and collect more data.
Identify Confusing Parts	Knowing what they don't understand while reading. Pinpointing parts that don't make sense is the step that precedes applying a helpful strategy.
Pause Then Retell or Summarize	Coping with the information in books by evaluating whether they recall details.
Self-Question	Setting purposes and creating interest while they read by posing questions, then reading to explore answers.
Self-Monitor	Knowing what is and is not understood. Seeking help when they cannot solve a problem independently.
Use Knowledge of Genres	Accessing what they already know about text structures to support the meaning-making process.
Synthesize	Summarizing information from large sections of a text. In their own words, as they read, students create a topic sentence and list the important details.
Determine What's Important	Selecting the important information in a chapter or section. Knowing what's relevant and what's irrelevant is crucial to comprehension and reading for a purpose.
Make Connections to Community	Engaging in analogous thinking by linking themes in a completed book to other books, to issues in their family, school, neighborhood, and the world.

Checklists for Monitoring Students' Reading

Before using the checklists on pages 47–55, read them carefully and decide which ones you feel will best monitor your students' attitudes toward reading, use of reading strategies, participation in partner and group book discussions, and knowledge of story structure.

Complete checklists you've selected twice a year for grade-level and proficient readers; for students who struggle, complete checklists you've selected every six to eight weeks—more if you feel this is appropriate. One checklist can last the year if you date observations and/or record them with different colored pens. If you are regularly kid-watching and noting your observations, you'll use the collected data and brief conferences to complete the checklists.

As I rotate among pairs and groups who are discussing a book, I focus on one to two students and complete the checklist. Since I also invite students to self-evaluate their book discussions (see pages 83–84), I monitor every students' participation twice a year, and study those who are consistently unprepared or rarely share ideas.

Complete the prediction and vocabulary checklists using journal entries and/or observations as students practice these strategies with short texts and their free-choice reading books, both at their independent reading levels. When I haven't collected enough observational notes to complete the prediction and vocabulary checklist, I hold a brief conference and invite students to show me how they apply specific strategies. Use checklists during student and parent conferences.

Throughout the year, you'll have multiple opportunities to monitor students' independent reading

- by studying their reading log (pages 87–88);
- through oral and written book reviews;
- by examining journal entries and critical paragraphs; and
- in one-on-one book conferences.

As you collect and review data, complete parts of the sheet and date your notes.

I completed this reading strategy checklist after observing a sixth grader.

CHECKLIST OF STRATEGIES STUDENTS USE WHILE READING

Name Robbie Z.   Observation Date_____

Strategies While Reading	Behaviors Readers are actively involved with texts.	Notes
Reading Rate	Adjusts rate with purposes such as skimming, reading to recall, reading for pleasure.	yes - tends to really slow down in science + history. books are too hard.
Predict/Support Confirm/Adjust	Supports predictions with text. Uses prior knowledge to confirm and adjust while reading.	yes
Question	Raises questions while reading. Knows that the text might not answer all questions.	yes
Self-Corrects	Knows when a word or phrase doesn't make sense and is able to correct without help. Has strategies to pronounce tough words.	work with roots + affixes will help this - he does know when a word is new + rereads + looks for clues. Not always finding a clue.
Monitors Understanding	Can identify parts of a text that are and aren't understood.	yes
Reread	Rereads to improve recall, to revisit favorite parts, and to understand confusing parts.	yes
Read/Pause/Summarize	Stops to check recall.	not always

Additional Comments and Notes:
group mini-lesson

Many strengths - does monitor reading - needs word meaning strategies + what to do when context doesn't work

Checklist of Strategies Students Use Before Reading

Student's Name _____ Observation Date _____

Before-Reading Strategies	Behaviors That Indicate Student Is Using Strategy	Notes
Brainstorm, Cluster, Fast-Write, Web, K-W-H-L, List	Activates prior knowledge and experiences to make them accessible during reading.	
Predict	Uses pictures, the title, and some text to support predictions.	
Skim	Reads captions, boldface headings, words, charts, and graphs to familiarize self with material.	
Question	Uses pictures, chapter headings, boldface headings and words, captions, graphs, and charts to generate meaningful questions.	
Predict Meaning Of New Vocabulary	Uses knowledge of roots, prefixes, and suffixes to predict meanings. Takes risks. Has broad word knowledge.	
Visualize	Creates mental pictures of words, concepts, and predictions.	
Set Purposes	Creates specific purposes for reading.	

Additional Comments and Notes:

Checklist of Strategies Students Use While Reading

Student's Name _____ Observation Date _____

During-Reading Strategies	Behaviors That Indicate Student Is Using Strategy	Notes
Adjust Reading Rate	Adjusts rate with purposes such as skimming, reading to recall, reading for pleasure.	
Predict/Support Confirm/Adjust	Supports predictions with text. Uses prior knowledge to confirm and adjust while reading.	
Question	Raises questions while reading. Knows that the text might not answer all questions.	
Self-Correct	Knows when a word or phrase doesn't make sense and is able to correct without help. Has strategies to pronounce tough words.	
Monitor Understanding	Can identify parts of a text that are and aren't understood.	
Reread	Rereads to improve recall, to revisit favorite parts, and to understand confusing parts.	
Read/Pause/ Summarize	Stops to check recall.	

Additional Comments and Notes:

Checklist of Strategies Students Use After Reading

Student's Name _____ Observation Date _____

After-Reading Strategies	Behaviors That Indicate Student Is Using Strategy	Notes
Confirm/Adjust Predictions	Uses specific text details to adjust predictions.	
Retell	Orally or in writing, uses details to retell story. Sequences events.	
Skim and Reread	Returns to text to prove points during discussions and for written responses.	
Take Notes	Can independently note important parts.	
Make Inferences	Uses dialogue, settings, conflicts, plot, characters' decisions, and facts to explore implied meanings.	
Reflect on Reading	Draws, talks, and writes about reading.	

Additional Comments and Notes:

Reading Checklist: Behaviors and Attitudes

Name _____

Key: R=Rarely; S=Sometimes; U=Usually; NO=Not Observed

Observed	Date	Additional Comments

LISTENING BEHAVIORS

___ Watches mini-lessons.

___ Listens during group discussions.

___ Can disagree without disrupting the discussion.

___ Makes eye contact.

___ Follows verbal directions.

SILENT READING/ENJOYMENT

___ Quickly settles down and reads.

___ Focuses on reading task.

___ Reads silently, without sub-vocalizing or whispering words.

___ Can get lost in a book.

___ Chooses books on different topics and genres.

___ Responds with emotions while reading: laughs, smiles, cries.

___ Chooses to read during free-choice time.

___ Discusses books with peers.

Additional Notes:

Story Elements and Interpretations Checklist

Name _____

Key: R=Rarely; S=Sometimes; U=Usually; NO=Not Observed

Observed	**Date**	**Additional Comments**

UNDERSTANDING OF STORY ELEMENTS

___ Understands the elements of realistic fiction.

___ Understands the elements of fantasy.

___ Understands the elements of science fiction.

___ Understands the elements of _____ (genre).

UNDERSTANDING OF NARRATIVE ELEMENTS

___ setting

___ protagonists

___ antagonists

___ mood

___ events

___ symbolism

___ conflicts

___ foreshadowing

___ flashback

___ time

CRITICAL THINKING/INTERPRETATION

___ Makes reasonable predictions about what will happen.

___ Uses examples from text to support predictions.

___ Adjusts predictions during and after reading.

___ Makes inferences.

___ Understands cause and effect.

___ Compares and contrasts characters and events.

___ Describes characters' traits using text as support.

___ Identifies themes or main points.

___ Discusses why a character changes.

___ Takes risks by trying out ideas with classmates.

___ Accepts that a book can have different interpretations.

Additional Notes:

Evaluation of Partner and Group Discussions

Student's Name _____ Observation Date _____

Key: R=Rarely; S=Sometimes; U=Usually; NO=Not Observed

PREPARATION

____ Brought book and materials.

____ Brought response journal.

____ Completed assignment.

____ Contributed to group work plan.

PARTICIPATION

____ Contributes to discussion.

____ Listens without interrupting.

____ Values diverse ideas.

____ Uses text for support.

____ Rereads to point to details.

____ Uses information from other source.

____ Gets involved in discussion.

____ Shares ideas and cooperates.

____ Uses prior knowledge/experiences for support.

____ Addresses ideas presented by peers.

____ Asks meaningful questions.

____ Can help keep discussion flowing.

____ Takes notes at appropriate times.

INTERPRETATION OF MATERIALS

____ Talks about story, problem, or graph.

____ Moves beyond "I like" or "I don't like."

____ Uses pictures and graphs to discover meaning.

____ Makes reasonable predictions.

____ Offers personal connections.

____ Can consider and search out alternate interpretations.

STORY STRUCTURE

____ Can talk meaningfully about plot, setting, characters, time, conflict, mood, dialogue, figurative language.

____ Uses structural elements in discussion.

Additional Notes and Comments:

Prediction Strategy Checklist

Name _____ Date _____

Title _____ Author _____

Key: R=Rarely; S=Sometimes; U=Usually; NO=Not Observed

BEFORE READING

____ Uses title and cover as support.

____ Uses knowledge of how stories work.

____ Uses own experiences.

____ Can select text that supports predictions.

____ Can differentiate between predictions based on text and predictions based on personal experiences.

____ Understands that predictions can be off target at this point.

DURING READING

____ Uses the story to support predictions.

____ Predicts more logically as more of the story is read.

____ Uses predictions to continue to create a need to read on and find out.

AFTER READING

____ Rereads to adjust predictions.

____ Uses story to support adjustments.

____ Confirms those predictions that were on target.

Strengths: Needs:

Student's Comments:

Negotiated Goal(s):

Vocabulary Checklist of Strategies

Name _____ Date _____

BEFORE READING

____ Previews boldface words.

____ Engages in preteaching experiences.

____ Studies illustrations, diagrams, photographs, and charts.

____ Records new words in journal.

DURING READING

____ Uses clues authors embed in text.

____ Rereads.

____ Reads sentences that came before and/or after the tough word or phrase.

____ Uses knowledge of the meaning of prefixes.

____ Uses knowledge of the meanings of Greek and Latin roots.

PRONOUNCING UNFAMILIAR WORDS

____ Looks at the beginning, middle, and end of word.

____ Removes suffix and prefix and studies root.

____ Looks for small, familiar words within a word.

____ Thinks of other words the tough word resembles.

____ Recognizes familiar word patterns.

____ Rereads.

____ Asks a peer for support.

____ Uses the dictionary.

AFTER READING

____ Uses the word correctly while speaking.

____ Includes the word in writing.

____ Finds synonyms and/or antonyms.

Additional Comments:

Checklist for Monitoring Independent Reading

Name _____ Date _____

Observations	Teacher's Notes

Observations

BOOK LOG ENTRIES

    Number of books

    Variety of titles

INDEPENDENT READING

    Selects books on independent level.

    Gets started quickly.

    Self-helps before seeking peer or teacher assistance.

    Shows pleasure in reading through journal entries, talk, and projects.

WRITTEN WORK

    Book reviews

    Critical paragraphs, essays

    Projects

    Dialogue journals

ORAL WORK

    Book talks, reviews

    Reading fluency

    Oral reading error patterns

Additional Notes and Questions:

Monitoring Students' Oral Reading

During the first two months of school, listen to each student read orally and record their errors, also called miscues, using the form on page 59. I start this process with a passage from students' independent reading books. If the passage is too difficult or too easy, then I listen to the student read from a more or less challenging title. The rest of the class reads silently, works on a journal entry, or quietly discusses a book.

The purpose of listening to students' oral reading is to determine their fluency and the kinds of errors or miscues they are making. You'll be listening for and noting omitted words, substituted words, repetitions, words students can't pronounce, and whether students pause for punctuation or read through it.

You can also ask students to retell passages you've used for error analysis as long as these are on their independent reading level. Take notes on the quality of their retellings (see pages 60–61). Retellings let you know how much students comprehend and recall and whether they can sequence events. It's helpful to ask students to reread a sentence or short passage and use context clues to explain the meaning of a challenging word. Students' independent reading books are also ideal for asking them to retell a short selection of one or several chapters.

It usually takes ten to fifteen minutes to hear students read a two-hundred word passage at their independent and instructional levels. Completing the Oral Reading Conference Checklist on page 59 helps me estimate students' instructional and independent reading levels. If I'm fortunate, last year's teacher will have passed this information to me. I ask students to bring their free-reading book to our first oral reading conference, as I've already shown them how to find a book that's just right. However, I also bring two books or two passages from a graded basal and photocopy one passage that is about a year below and another one year above the student's book. This way, I avoid derailing a meeting, for if the student's book is too easy or too difficult, I can use one of the passages I brought.

Meet in a quiet corner. Explain the purpose of these assessment meetings to everyone, so students working independently understand why you're asking for their cooperation.

The Three Cueing Systems

Readers use a variety of cues or signals embedded in text to decipher unknown words or difficult passages (Gillet and Temple, 1990). A knowledge of these cueing systems will enable you to better analyze students' miscues and decide how to help your students obtain effective strategies for coping with tough words and passages.

Graphophonic: This refers to the relationship between the letters in a word and the sounds they make. It's helpful to determine if readers are missing, and not self-correcting, the letter-sound relationships at the beginning, middle, or ends of words. Or are they substituting words that have no sounds in common, such as *this* for *every*? You can support students who consistently don't attend to specific parts of words through word sorting, studying word parts such as prefixes, suffixes, and roots. A great resource for word sorting activities is *Words Their Way: Word Study for Phonics, Vocabulary, and Spelling Instruction* by Bear, Invernizzi, Johnston, and Templeton, Merrill, 1996, revised edition, 1999.

Syntactic: This grammar-related cueing system has to do with how language works and the order of words in a sentence. An example of a syntactic miscue is when the reader substitutes a word that is a different part of speech or a non-word. For example, the text reads: *The girl cried for hours.* The student reads: *The girl sad for hours.* Here the student substituted an adjective, *sad*, for the verb *cried*.

Possible Interventions:
- Repair strategies can include improving students' understanding of sentence structure by focusing their attention on difficult sentences (Barr, et al., 1990).
- These strategies can improve deficits in syntax:
  — Read aloud daily, so students hear literary language;
  — Encourage students to read a variety of genres;
  — Offer many opportunities for students to write, speak, and listen.
- Hearing and using language will develop competence with the syntactic cueing system.

Semantic: These cues are meaning-related. Meaning-related miscues spotlight the reader's ability to attend to the meaning of the text. Yetta Goodman, et al. (1995), point out that many miscues do not affect or impede comprehension. However, readers who make many substitutions need to have their attention called to the structure of the word and the letter-sound relationships. Subtle differences in meaning can occur when a student reads *laughed* for *snickered* or *fussed* for *fumed*. Therefore, offer repair strategies to students whose miscues change the meaning of a passage and to those who repeatedly substitute words with similar meanings. Word sorting, analysis of word parts, webbing words related to a root, and a comparison of the letters of the word in the text with the substituted word are effective reading repair strategies.

Interpreting Students' Oral Reading

1. Repetitions, hesitations, reading through punctuation, and self-correcting are not counted as errors. However, if a student reads a short passage with many of the above errors and a sketchy retelling, he or she might be in a passage that's too difficult and/or requires support with fluency (see page 58 for suggestions).
2. Omitting words, inserting new words, substituting words, and telling a student how to

pronounce a word are all counted as errors.

3. Students who make ten or more errors every one hundred words are at their frustration level; the passage is too difficult.

4. Students who make one to five errors every one hundred words and retell with about 75 percent comprehension are at their instructional level.

5. Students who make one to two errors every one hundred words and retell with excellent comprehension are at their independent level. Sometimes a students might retell the passage in great detail but make three to five errors. Use your judgment and knowledge of the student to decide whether this is his or her independent or instructional level.

For fluent readers who retell with rich details, this start-of-the-year read-aloud conference is enough. For students who lack fluency, offer them opportunities to develop fluency and repeat the conference every six to eight weeks; use results to point out progress and improvement to students. Disfluent readers expend their energy decoding words and often have difficulty recalling details and connecting what they know to the text, which seriously hampers comprehension.

Suggestions for Developing Reading Fluency

Here are some strategies for helping students develop reading fluency. *Always use materials at students' independent-reading levels.*

Repeated Readings: Invite students to reread a sentence, several sentences or a paragraph until the reading is fluent and with expression. It's helpful for the teacher to read first, and then to ask the student to imitate the expression, rhythm, and inflection.

Echo-Read Poetry: The teacher reads one or two lines, then the student reads the same lines, imitating the teacher.

Memorize Poetry: Ask students to read a poem many times, memorize it, then recite it to classmates or to younger students.

Present Short Plays or Readers' Theater Scripts: Students choose characters, read the play silently, and discuss the personality of their character. Have students reread and practice their parts until they can project character with their voices. Groups present plays to their class or to younger students.

Tape-Record Reading: Invite students to tape an early reading and a later reading of the same passage. Between readings, have students reread the passage until they have gained fluency. Students compare readings and discuss how they achieved fluency and improved comprehension.

Make Audiocassettes For Younger Students: Have a primary teacher invite older students to prepare tapes for listening centers. Older students practice reading their books until they've achieved fluency and tape these. At a listening center, younger students use the audiocassettes.

Oral Reading Conference Checklist

Name _____ Date _____

Title/Author _____ Pages Read _____

Observations	Notes and Examples
Reads fluently, with expression, and in meaningful chunks.	
Phrases reading within punctuation marks.	
Ignores punctuation. [Note how many times this occurred.]	
Frequently hesitates before words. [Write words, page, and paragraph.]	
Struggles pronouncing multisyllabic words. [List the words.]	
Repeats words, phrases many times. [Note repeated words, phrases.]	
Needs frequent prompting on words. [List the words you helped student pronounce.]	
Makes word substitutions. [Write text word and substituted word.]	
Omits words. [List omitted words and the word that comes after each omitted word.]	

Additional comments:

The Retelling Checklist: Narrative

PURPOSE:
To evaluate students recall and their ability
to include rich details told in sequence.

When you invite students to retell a passage or chapter at their instructional and/or independent reading level, you gather information about their ability to recall, comprehend, sequence details, and make personal connections. As students retell, they put the text into their own words, organizing ideas and recalling relevant details.

It's helpful to prompt students before and after retellings.

Open with: *Take some time to think about the passage. Recall everything you remember, and I will record your words.*

After student stops, ask: *Can you recall more details?* or *Would you like to add anything?* (If the student asks you to read back the dictated retelling, do so and make a note of the request.)

Use the form on page 61, which helps you note and evaluate students' retellings. Those who offer rich, detailed retellings can read independently while you scaffold students who require additional support. Students who can retell in great detail are probably ready to learn how to summarize by selecting four to six key points in a chapter or long passage and organizing these into a short paragraph.

If students experience difficulty with retelling, the text might be too difficult, filled with many new words, or they might have little to no prior knowledge of the topic. Scaffold students' retellings by having them read then retell one to two sentences. Once students can do this, gradually increase the length of the text that they retell.

As a sixth grader retold the first two chapters of Bridge to Terabithia, I filled out this checklist.

RETELLING CHECKLIST: NARRATIVE

Student's Name _Sandra B._ _____ Date___

Record of Student's Retelling: Chapters 1 & 2 - Bridge to Terabithia
- Rich details
- Spoke confidently
- Loves the book - can't stop reading it
- Like K.P.'s language - "mad as flies in a fruit jar."

Elements in Student's Retelling	Teacher's Notes
Identified Main Character	In detail
Told Main Character's Problem	Several - wants to stay fastest kid - sisters - older - drawing - dad dislikes
Settings: Time and Place	So far - Jess's house
Rising Action: Plot Details	Good details - some out of order - but fixed
Mentioned Other Characters	All so far

Student's Speaking Patterns: Answer *yes* or *no*. Give examples when important.

Spoke in complete sentences. _yes_

Told details in chronological order. _not all - backtracked to correct_

Added details when you asked for more. _yes_

Additional Comments:
- Book is perfect for Sandra. She "rereads" to keep plot in her head.
- Made connections - She's like Maybelle - the youngest - she has 2 older sisters but they're not as nice as Jesse.
- Pleased that Sandra is taking her favorite phrases and writing them in her note book.

Retelling Checklist: Narrative

Student's Name _____ Date _____

Record of Student's Retelling:

Elements in Student's Retelling	Teacher's Notes
Identified Main Character	
Told Main Character's Problem	
Settings: Time and Place	
Rising Action: Plot Details	
Mentioned Other Characters	

Student's Speaking Patterns: Answered *yes* or *no*. Gave examples when important.

_____ Spoke in complete sentences.

_____ Told details in chronological order.

_____ Added details when asked for more.

Additional Comments:

Partner and Group Observation Record

PURPOSE:
To reinforce productive work behaviors; to negotiate goals with students.

When you observe students as they work in pairs or groups, you can reinforce productive behaviors with a follow-up teacher observation conference with one or more groups or the entire class. Through frequent observations, you'll sharpen your kid-watching and note-taking skills. You'll also teach students to be self-evaluative about their abilities to stay on task, interact with a partner or group, and value the way others think.

Make an overhead transparency of the form on page 63, carry it on a clipboard, jot your notes, and quickly share with the class. File transparencies in a folder and refer back to them to show students their progress.

To prepare for this conference, circulate, watch, listen, and note all the positive behaviors and interactions (see form on page 63). Jot down one to three areas that you feel could improve. About twelve to fifteen minutes before the end of the period do the following:

- Read the notes aloud.
- Invite students to discuss them.
- Add observations students recalled that weren't on your list.
- Ask students which need they believe should be their short-term goal; have students suggest others they feel are important.

It's helpful to observe the same learning experience two to three weeks later and compare notes, highlighting students' progress. As you share and discuss observations students sharpen their ability to: Reflect, Listen, Question, Evaluate, and Negotiate Goals.

PARTNER & GROUP OBSERVATION RECORD

Date _Dec. 7, 1998_ Observation of _Class organized in Groups- Book Discussions_

List Strengths:
- On task
- all brought books, journals, pencils
- Questions asked to clarify point
- Many read from book to prove point
- Heard students ask for support
- Group leaders used prompts to keep discussion going
- Many took notes
- All wrote summaries of high points at end.

List Needs:
- Too loud — flicked lights to quiet down.
- Argued when a group member disagreed.
- Several did not participate

Negotiated Goal:
- Value others' ideas - discuss in quiet voice

This Partner and Group Observation Record helped me identify needs and set goals for this group of fifth graders.

Partner and Group Observation Record

Date _____   Observation of _____

List Strengths:

List Needs:

Negotiated Goal:

Teacher-Student
Reading Conference Form

PURPOSE:
To prepare for conferences so they remain short and focused; to collect notes that can help you decide on supportive intervention.

FORMS THAT HELP YOU OBSERVE STUDENTS

Keeping teacher-student conferences to five to twelve minutes allows you to confer with two to four students a day and meet the needs of many. This means that you will need to focus the conference topic and address one issue that you or the student raises. Sometimes I suggest two topics and ask the student to choose one. Other times I invite the student to suggest the topic, and keep one in mind just in case the student has no ideas. Students don't become overwhelmed with a limited focus because they think of one problem, not several. Moreover, limiting the time and number of topics reduces teachers' frustration and anxiety and eliminates a snaking line of students waiting for their turn.

During a focus conference, ask questions, listen carefully, and watch how students apply or talk about applying a reading strategy. Sometimes you'll have time to offer practical suggestions. If not, determine how to help the student—with individual activities, group work, or further one-on-one time with you.

Record comments—both yours and those made by the student—on the form on page 65. Often, I prepare for these brief meetings and list the topic up for discussion and points I wish to make. This frees me to be a better listener. Have students store these notes in their response journal, making the information available to students when they apply a reading strategy or respond to a book.

Teacher-Student Reading Conference Form

Name _Latisha C._ Date _Jan. 13, 1999_

Topic to be Discussed: _Selecting key details_

Points Discussed by Teacher and Student:
- Set a purpose or use purpose group set.
- Think about purpose.
- Select details that relate to purpose.

Teacher Recommendations:
- Put purpose on Post-it.
- Reread purpose when selecting details & jotting these on Post-its.

Actions/Goals Student and Teacher Negotiated:
- Latisha practiced with me by her side.
- Prompting from me helped.
- Set up mini-practices over next 2 days

Follow-up Conference Needed? _yes_ Date _Jan. 20_
Additional Comments:
Have Latisha work with Marie when selecting key details

I filled out this form immediately after meeting with Latisha, an eighth grader, about her reading.

Teacher-Student Reading Conference Form

Name _____ Date _____

Topic to Be Discussed:

Points Discussed by Teacher and Student:

Teacher Recommendations:

Actions/Goals Student and Teacher Negotiated:

Follow-Up Conference Needed? _____ Date _____

Additional Comments:

Rubric for Journal Entries

Journal responses are a great way to gain insight into students' levels of comprehension, their ability to connect books to their lives, other books, community and world issues, and how well they can select story details to support an idea.

Model how you set up a journal page and respond to a prompt. Reserve time for the class to collaborate with you and for pairs to practice before moving students to independence. Observing your process demystifies the assignment and results in better student work.

Setting guidelines that outline expectations for journal entries enables students to evaluate their work against a set of reasonable standards. Adapt the journal rubric on page 67 to your goals.

Some Easy-to-Introduce Journal Responses

- Identify the main character, list several problems he or she faces, and explain how the problem was solved. If the problem wasn't solved, explain why and tell how you might have solved it.
- Summarize and evaluate two to three decisions the main character made.
- Select an important quote from the story (one to three sentences), explain how you connected to the quote, and show how the quote relates to a theme, conflict, or character in the text.
- Select three key events and show how each provided insight into a character's personality.
- List several things that you value or are important to you. List what your favorite character values. Compare and contrast lists, pointing out what you have in common and how you differ.
- Visualize a scene or a character; use drawings or words to illustrate these.
- Choose a minor character and show how he or she was important to the plot, main character, or themes.

The teacher or students can use the rubric on page 67 to score journal entries. If you score the entry, use the rubric to comment on student's work. Remember to start with positives.

Four-Point Rubric for Journal Entries

Score 4 Points:
★ Includes several supporting details from the text.

★ Makes personal connections and/or connections to other books.

★ Follows directions carefully.

★ Makes inferences using story details.

Score 3 Points:
★ Includes one to two supporting details.

★ Makes a personal connection.

★ Follows most of the directions.

Score 2 Points:
★ Retells the story.

★ Makes a personal connection.

★ Follows a few directions.

Score 1 Point:
★ Retells the story.

★ Does not follow the directions.

Interpreting the Data You've Collected

Every four to six weeks, review the assessment data in students' literacy folders for struggling readers, for these are the students who continually require scaffolding to improve. With a class of 25 to 35 students, I recommend evaluating solid readers every ten to twelve weeks because they also need encouragement and attention and support to move forward. Moreover, you'll want to deepen their ability to infer, explore themes, and understand fiction and nonfiction structures. Once you've reviewed data, staple or clip the pages together so you can quickly locate new information and, if necessary, review the old.

Though it's tempting to offer students support for several reading strategies, I have found that too many suggestions confuse and frustrate students while raising teachers' anxiety levels. Here are some questions that will enable you to narrow your evaluation focus:

- Do I want to evaluate a strategy the student has been practicing?
- Do I want to review the student's progress with a recently introduced strategy?
- Has the student requested support or shown that he or she needs support with a specific strategy?
- If the student needs scaffolding with several strategies, which is the most important one to evaluate?

Use the chart on page 69 that lists specific learning events in a reading workshop and a range of assessments that can help you monitor these events. The chart includes possible assessments that you can choose from as you decide whether to scaffold students' reading in one-on-one conferences or in small groups of two to three students.

Assessing Students' Reading

Reading Experience	Possible Assessments
Determining Student's View of Self as Reader	Interviews; What's Easy? What's Hard? reading and interest surveys; all-about-me letters; observational notes
Reading for Strategies	Oral reading; miscue patterns; guided reading groups; debriefing; conferences; self-evaluations; checklists; response to mini-lessons; interviews
Selecting a Book	Book logs; journal entries; oral reading; retellings; book conferences; book talks; observational notes
Reading Out Loud	Error or miscue analysis; taped recording for fluency; Readers' Theater (See *Teaching Reading in Middle School* by Laura Robb, Scholastic, 2000.)
Understanding What You Read	One-on-one conference; journal entries; book discussions; book talks; book reviews; critical essays; tests; quizzes; strategic reading groups
Choosing Books for Free Reading	Book logs; journal entries; book conferences; book reviews; book discussions; observational notes
Self-Evaluating Progress	Checklists; narratives that analyze progress over time; debriefings

FORMS THAT HELP YOU OBSERVE STUDENTS

Evaluate, Interpret, Plan, Teach

Student's Name _____ Date _____

Focus of evaluation:

List key points from collected data:

List any questions the review of data raised:

Note some possible interventions:

Check one:

_____ Small-group meetings:

_____ One-on-one meetings:

Additional Comments:

Tips for Transforming Assessments
Into Interventions

Here is a summary of my process. Use it as a starting point or let it spark ways you can adapt what I do to your teaching style.

Review Literacy Folder: Reread observational notes, sample journal entries, checklists, and any other assessments in the folder. Concentrate on the issue you believe will benefit the student the most.

Determine the Focus of Evaluating Assessments: Select one strategy or problem to focus on; otherwise both you and the student will feel overwhelmed. The focus might be a reading strategy you're presently working on, an issue that the student has been struggling with for several weeks, or a broadening of the student's range of free-reading choices.

Note Key Points That Relate to Focus: Jot down issues that relate to the focus. You'll collect these by reviewing the literacy folder and from your knowledge of a reading strategy. For example, if I'm going to help a student move from retelling to summarizing, a related issue is the ability to select key details and set aside less important ones.

Raise Questions: Asking questions helps me move closer to thinking of possible ways to scaffold a strategy. Sometimes I revisit the scaffolding suggestions on pages 15–20, as rereading those often generates ideas in my mind or provides me with two or three interventions.

Propose Possible Interventions: Try to list more than one way to intervene. Quite often, I have to abandon one way of scaffolding for another because the second is more effective for a particular student.

Confer With Student: Take three to four minutes to let the student know what you've discovered by reviewing his or her literacy folder; explain your support plan.

See an example of this process using the Evaluate, Interpret, Intervene form on the next page.

Consider my notes on Tamika's literacy folder, shown below. Tamika struggles with reading, even at her independent level. She is one of six students that I am monitoring closely because they require scaffolding to improve. Note how the original focus of "reading rate" enlarges as I move through the evaluating process to possible interventions. Taking notes involves time, but jotting notes generates ideas that I believe are important to record.

When I first started this process, I needed fifteen to twenty minutes per student. Over the years, through practice and by reading professional books and journals to enlarge my knowledge base, I have shortened the time to ten to twelve minutes. If you're just starting this process, I suggest you only focus on your most needy readers until you gain confidence, background knowledge about reading, and speed. This might take two to five years and that's fine.

EVALUATE, INTERPRET, INTERVENE

Student's Name _Tamika_____ Date _Nov. 3, 1999_

Focus of Evaluation: _Reading Rate - Slow down_

List key points from collected data:
- 1st finished in class
- discussions show sketchy recall
- Tamika wrote: "reading fast means you're smart"
- Doesn't reread + says - "Don't remember" a lot
- On "What's Hard" - answering questions in history, science doesn't like reading - says it's boring
- Workshop self-evaluation - finishes fast

List any questions, the review of data raised: ?
- Is this a prior knowledge problem too?
- Should I have a whole-class/small group mini-lesson on reading rate?
- What info will science + history teacher give?
- should I include rereading in intervention?
- What about Read/Pause/Retell strategy?

Note some possible interventions:
- several one-on-ones -
- work on prior knowledge, slowing down -
- use Post-its to jot reactions, details

Check one:
_Small group meetings

✓One-on-one meetings: ask Tamika questions that might give info on prior knowledge

Additional Comments: group Tamika with the 4 you're working on using post-its to respond, reread + discuss.

My notes on my review of Tamika's literacy folder.

Part 4

When Students Self-Evaluate

Near the end of the school year, after students have had lots of practice self-evaluating their reading, I invite students to reread their self-evaluations, then reflect on and respond to these prompts: "I used to... Now I can..." The sample responses that follow illustrate how empowering this experience can be.

I used to hate reading and never finished a book. Now I can find a book I like and can read.
— Fifth Grader

I used to think that all reading was boring. Now I can't wait to read all the Animorph books.
— Seventh Grader

I used to think that the smart kids had strategies just because they were smart. Now I can predict and find support and think of the important ideas. — Eighth Grader

Not all students make dramatic turnarounds, and it's important to temper your expectations. The statements that follow are from students who still felt as discouraged at the end of the year. However, I try to think of their year with me as a small beginning, and that other teachers will continue supporting them and the changeover will eventually arrive.

I used to think reading was pointless and I still do, even if I can read some of the books.
— Sixth Grader

I used to not have any strategies to help with reading. I learned some strategies that help, but I still don't like to read. — Eighth Grader

Even the negative self-evaluations are useful, for I pass these along to students' new teachers. My hope is that the teachers will understand the frustration and anxiety these young adolescents experience and continue to nurture and support each one.

For self-evaluation to affect students' learning, it should encompass their academic experiences, goals, and behavior during workshop. The forms in this section invite students to think about these three aspects of their learning. As you read students' self-evaluations, consider these guidelines:

- Connect students' perspectives to your observations.
- Meet with other colleagues who teach the student and compare their observations with yours and the student's.
- Evaluate students' goals with them to make sure they are reasonable.
- Use students' self-evaluations to adjust classroom practices when appropriate.
- Help students focus on positives and see the progress you've observed.

Keep in mind that communicating with students does not always translate into positive change. I have learned to accept students' negative and/or angry comments as cries for help, not personal attacks on me. Try to move beyond those initial reactions and angry thoughts to asking yourself, *How can I use this information to support this student?*

Self evaluations help students—and you—see their progress in reading and identify goals to work toward.

Self-Evaluation Checklist for the Predict-and-Support Strategy

PURPOSE:
To encourage students to self-monitor their progress and negotiate meaningful goals with the teacher.

Invite students to complete this checklist after they have practiced and independently used the predict/support/confirm or adjust strategy. Do this two to three times a year.

Before completing the checklist, I like students to reread their most recent piece of independent work in which they've applied this strategy to a free-choice reading book. Have students attach their work to the self-evaluation form on page 76. When you read the checklist, it's helpful to have the work the student used to self-evaluate so you can comment and make supportive recommendations.

Meet with the student for three to five minutes, review the checklist, note student's comments, and together negotiate a goal. While students read independently or work on a journal entry, I circulate, return self-evaluations, and have a brief chat. In twenty minutes, I can visit with five to eight students and return all of the checklists over five days. I spend more time conferring with struggling readers than with strong readers.

Place checklists in students' literacy folders and ask students to note their goal on a page in their journal reserved for recording goals. Next time students apply the predict/support strategy, ask them to review their goal and note it under "Student's Comments," then decide if they have achieved the goal.

Middle school teachers who have four to five English classes can stagger the scheduling of these checklists so they aren't overwhelmed with reading more than 140 papers.

SELF-EVALUATION CHECKLIST FOR PREDICT AND SUPPORT

Name _Sam T. (Samantha)_ Date _Oct. 28, 1998_

Title and Author _Parks Quest – K. Paterson_

Directions: This checklist will help you think about the way you made predictions about the characters and events in the book. After you read each item, place a check next to items you included as you predicted and supported; leave others blank.

After Completing Chapter 1
- ✓ I used the title and cover as support.
- ✓ I used the information in the first chapter as support.
- ___ I used my own knowledge of how stories work.
- ___ I used my own experiences to support predictions.
- ✓ Predicting made me want to continue the book.
- ✓ At this point, my predictions could be off target.

Halfway Through the Book
- ✓ My prediction was based on what had already happened.
- ___ I used examples from the story as support.
- ✓ I find myself predicting as I read more and more of the story.
- ___ Making predictions makes the reading enjoyable.

After Completing the Book
- ___ I reread parts of the book so I could adjust off-target predictions.
- ___ I gave examples from the story to support my adjustments.
- ✓ I confirmed predictions that were on target.

Student's Comments: _I forgot to predict when I get into the story. I go past the first list and keep reading._

Teacher's Comments and Recommendations _Next book Sam and I will complete the P+S Post-its together._

Student's Goal for the Next Book: _To remember what to do – stop and write my prediction and support._

A sixth grader completed this self-evaluation after reading Parks Quest *and set a reading goal for her next book.*

Self-Evaluation Checklist for the Predict-and-Support Strategy

Name _____ Date _____

Title and Author _____

Directions: This checklist will help you think about the way you made predictions about the characters and events in the book. After you read each item, place a check next to the ones you used as you predicted and supported; leave others blank.

After Completing Chapter One

_____ I used the title and cover as support.

_____ I used the information in the first chapter as support.

_____ I used my own knowledge of how stories work.

_____ I used my own experiences to support predictions.

_____ Predicting made me want to continue the book.

_____ At this point, my predictions could be off target.

Halfway Through the Book

_____ My prediction was based on what had already happened.

_____ I used examples from the story as support.

_____ I found myself predicting as I read more and more of the story.

_____ Making predictions makes the reading enjoyable.

After Completing the Book

_____ I reread parts of the book so I could adjust off-target predictions.

_____ I gave examples from the story to support my adjustments.

_____ I confirmed predictions that were on target.

Student's Comments:

Teacher's Comments and Recommendations:

Student's Goal for the Next Book:

Peer Evaluation of Journal Form

PURPOSE:
To encourage peers to read one another's journals and observe how a classmate completed the assignment; to develop peer evaluation.

It took me several years to change the way I graded students' literature response journals. At first, every Friday, I'd stack students' journals in cartons, lug them to my car, and spend the weekend reading and reacting to each one. My husband and two children would hike, pick strawberries, visit a museum, or take in a movie. Not me. While my family enjoyed weekend time, I pored over students' journal entries.

As my desire to be part of these family excursions increased, I found a solution. Instead of reading every journal entry, sometimes I'd ask students to select one entry for me to read and I'd select one at random. By reading five journals each day over five school days, I eliminated hours of weekend work.

Then I decided that some of the journal evaluation should be turned over to students. The form on page 78 invites students to evaluate an entry I select or one that students choose. Vary who chooses the entry throughout the year. I discovered that when students peer-evaluate each other's work, their own work improves because they observe how classmates have thought about and responded to a prompt. "I thought it was cool the way Amy quoted from her book (James Clavell's *The Children's Story*, Bantam, Doubleday, Dell, 1981) to prove that the new teacher consciously tried to tear apart the children's respect for family, religion, and individuality. I think I'll try that next time," Cyrena wrote.

A sixth grader's evaluation of his peer's journal entry.

Journal Entry is on Traitor: The Story of Benedict Arnold by Jean Fritz. Question: Do you find a traitor more appealing than a hero?

PEER EVALUATION OF JOURNALS FORM

Directions: Read your partner's journal entry carefully, then respond.

I. Summarize, in two sentences, the content of this entry.

① Traitor more exciting - does daring things
② Fun to read about traitors - having to live with them is hard.

II. List all the good points about this entry. Think of the goal and guidelines of the assignment. In what ways did your classmate reach the goal?

Answered question
Used sentences.
Correct heading
neat - easy to read

III. Offer one to two suggestions for improving the content of this entry.

Can you give examples from the book? Very general entry.

IV. Did you learn anything about composing an entry? If yes, what?

neat writing is good.
Giving examples really prove the point.

Journal Writer's Name _Steve S._ Date _2/11/98_

Peer Partner's Name _Nick T_ Date _2/16/98_

Peer Evaluation of Journal Form

Directions: Read your partner's journal entry carefully, then respond.

1. Summarize in two sentences the content of this entry.

2. List all the good points about this entry. Think of the goal and guidelines of the assignment. In what ways did your classmate reach the goal?

3. Offer one to two suggestions for improving the content of this entry.

4. Did you learn anything about composing an entry? If yes, what?

Journal Writer's Name _____ Date _____

Peer Partner's Name _____ Date _____

35 MUST-HAVE ASSESSMENT AND RECORD-KEEPING FORMS FOR READING

Peer Book Conference Form

PURPOSE:
To teach students how to confer about books with each other.

For the first three to four months of school, I use this form for monthly, one-on-one book conferences with each student. From their book logs (see page 89), I alternate inviting students to choose a book completed during the month or to discuss one I select. These conferences, which I hold when the class reads or writes independently, provide students with a model and a common experience.

Before partners confer with one another, ask them to tell you what they have learned about book conferences. Use students' understandings to set conference guidelines; write them on chart paper. Here's a list sixth graders offered:

- Bring your book. You'll want to refer to it.
- Bring a pencil—you'll need it.
- Listen carefully so you can summarize the discussion.
- Ask questions that help your partner talk about the book.
- Take notes so you can remember—use the back of the form.
- Sometimes Mrs. R. chooses and other times we choose the book.

To the suggestions above, add these guidelines:
- The student who listens completes the form.
- Each student has five to ten minutes to discuss his or her book.
- The listener completes the form immediately after the conference.
- Students turn in the completed forms.

Filling out this Peer Book Conference form helped sixth grader Missy reflect on her discussion with Maylis and think more about the book.

Peer Book Conference

Our conference was on _____ between:

                              [date]

Name _____

Name _____

Title and Author _____

Check the focus of the conference:

_____ Retelling of a chapter or the entire story

_____ The main character's changes from beginning to end

_____ Problems the main character faced and how he or she dealt with them

_____ Conflicts and resolutions

_____ The character and/or situations the reader connected to, and why

_____ Discussion of the genre and the genre's structure

_____ Question(s). Note the question(s) discussed.

_____ Visualizing parts of the story

_____ Confirming and adjusting predictions

_____ Discussion of new information and new words the reader met

_____ The illustrations

_____ The settings

_____ Reactions to the ending or other parts of the book

Preparation checklist:

_____ I came with my book.

_____ I brought a pencil.

List the main points of the discussion:

35 MUST-HAVE ASSESSMENT AND RECORD-KEEPING FORMS FOR READING

Partner Book Conference Record Sheet

Student's Name _____

Partner's Name _____ Date _____

Title and Author of Partner's Book _____

Preparation Checklist: Came with _____ book _____ pencil

Tell the topic your partner talked about.

List two points your partner discussed.

Did your partner recommend the book to you? Explain why or why not.

Workshop Self-Evaluation Form

PURPOSE:
To encourage students to reflect on their use of choice time.

If social talk dominates choice experiences such as partner and group book discussions or independent reading, I invite students to think about their decisions and behavior and set a goal for the next workshop. Self-evaluation continues until I observe students working productively. Then I ask students to complete the form on page 83 every two to four weeks.

Before an independent workshop starts, students write what they hope to accomplish. At the end of the workshop, ask students to reread and evaluate these goals, and set new ones. Seventh-grader Jamal writes, "I meant to read a chapter in my book, then work on my persuasive essay. I didn't do them. I talked. I read some pieces in my writing folder. Tomorrow, I won't sit near Tony and try to do work." Like adults, middle school students have days when they don't feel like working. Confronting them with their own words enables me to deal with this issue without nagging and sounding judgmental. The next day, as I circulated among students, I asked Jamal to reread his self-evaluation and think about his goal for today's choice time. Jamal did read a chapter, but he lapsed into chatting with Josh for part of the time.

Accomplishing turnabouts is challenging and won't happen quickly. Sitting with a student or small group to help them organize their work, set reasonable goals, and support them as they read and write can help students learn to focus and be productive.

Workshop Self-Evaluation

Name Sue Ann L. Date 2/27/95

I plan to accomplish the following in today's workshop:
Rite 2 mor leeds.
Read

What did I accomplish?
I did all — And Mrs. Robb was pround of me

How can I use my work time to accomplish more?
stay in my seet and keep from talkin

Here are my goal(s) for next workshop class:
Write more detals in my story
I need to met with Mrs. Robb
Read more

A workshop self-evaluation helps middle school students monitor their own performance and develop responsibility. This fifth grader accurately recognizes what she needs to do to be more productive during workshop.

Workshop Self-Evaluation

Name _____ Date _____

I plan to accomplish the following in today's workshop:

What did I accomplish?

How can I use my work time to accomplish more?

Here are my goal(s) for next workshop class:

Students' Self-Evaluation Form for Book Discussions

PURPOSE:
To encourage students to self-monitor and evaluate their participation in partner and small group book discussions.

It's impossible for me to listen to more than one group discuss a book in a twenty-minute free-choice time. If pairs and groups of students are conversing during a forty-five minute period, I can visit, support, and evaluate two groups. Through November, I evaluate student participation (see page 85) during book discussions and share evaluations with individuals during brief conferences. This enables students to understand the evaluative process as well as experience and adjust the discussion standards they have negotiated with me. One standard I always negotiate is that students must come to their group prepared. If a student has not read the pages, then he or she reads in a quiet corner of the classroom, then joins the group.

As soon as I observe meaningful book discussions, I turn the evaluation process over to students. Often, this occurs before November, especially with classes who have had similar experiences.

Take the time to model how you would complete the form and the kind of comments you would add. Share student evaluations from the previous year and delete students' names so samples remain anonymous. Students' self-evaluations combined with the observational notes I take provide me with valuable information about individuals and how students have been paired and grouped—information I use to decide which group or pair requires additional support.

A seventh grader reflects on her participation in a book discussion group.

Student's Self-Evaluation Form
For Book Discussions

Name _____ Date _____

Criteria	Comments

Preparation:

_____ I brought the book and related materials.

_____ I read the appropriate section.

_____ I brought my journal and a pencil.

_____ I jotted notes for discussion.

Participation (give an example of each checked item):

_____ I made meaningful contributions.

_____ I listened to others without interrupting.

_____ I asked thoughtful questions.

_____ I used my book and/or materials to support ideas.

_____ I valued the contributions of others.

_____ I adjusted my responses when appropriate.

Behavior:

_____ I abided by guidelines the class set.

_____ I used my group discussion voice.

_____ I supported others.

_____ I talked about the task the group agreed upon.

_____ I helped keep the discussion going.

Peer Reading Strategy Conference Form

PURPOSE:
To enable students to learn how peers apply specific reading strategies; to encourage students to talk about reading strategies.

A superb way students can increase their knowledge of the reading strategies practiced and applied during workshop is through peer conferences that focus on a specific strategy such as questioning, activating prior knowledge, note-taking, or summarizing (see form on page 87).

The responses below illustrate how inviting students to confer about strategies they've practiced several times enables you to pinpoint students who understand a strategy and those who need additional practice and teacher support.

I'm never sure the notes I take from my history book are important. Tess says she folds her paper in half and writes a bold word or question on one side and phrases that answer it on the other side. —Seventh Grader

I like to predict but I hate to go back and reread everything to find support. I guess at support because the other takes too much time. —Fifth Grader

I think skimming is cool. I search for the place and only reread what I have to. Words in the question give me ideas of what to look up. —Fifth Grader

Summarizing is supposed to be short. I can't think of a few important things to put in my summary. I still tell everything. —Seventh Grader

I learned from David that asking questions keeps him interested. —Sixth Grader

Peer conferences tap into the social nature of middle school students. In addition, talking and writing can help pairs clarify their understandings and can deepen your insights about how students use a strategy.

Peer Reading Strategy Conference

Our conference was held on _____ between

[date]

Name _____

Name _____

Write the strategy you practiced and discussed:

List all the ways this strategy helped you:

What did you learn about the strategy from your partner?

What other strategies did you use along with the one you practiced?

Book Log Form

PURPOSE:
To construct a record of students' reading and their range of topics; to use this record during student conferences; to collect data that allows students to self-evaluate their independent reading.

"When my dad read my book log he was amazed that by January I had read twenty books. He said that he never read so much when he was in eighth grade. My dad asked why I was so interested in fantasy and sci-fi books. He asked me to pick one and said that he would read it, then we could talk about it." David's comments were part of his evaluation of his progress in reading (see pages 89–92) and reveal the benefits of maintaining book logs.

Parents enjoy reviewing book logs with students and, along with teachers, learn much about their child's interests and personal reading lives. Book logs can become the topic of short conferences in which you and students discuss the range and variety of reading, providing you with opportunities to suggest titles that can broaden students' interests.

When students ask, "Can I have another log sheet?" their voice always reveals a sense of pride and accomplishment in their reading. Pairs and groups enjoy exchanging book logs and jotting down titles classmates recommend.

Students can store book logs in their writing folders, literature response journals, or portfolios.

READING LOG

Title, Author	Date Completed
Libby on Wednesday by Zilpha Keatley Snyder	September 20, 1997
Twenty Ways to Lose your Best Friend by Marilyn Singer	September 24, 1997
Outrageously Alice by Phyllis Reynolds Naylor	October 7, 1997
Out of Control by Norma Fox Mazer	October 12, 1997
Uncanny! by Paul Jennings	November 9, 1997
Alice in Lace by Phyllis Reynolds Naylor	December 18, 1997
Upside Down by Mary Jane Miller	December 8, 1997
What Kind of Love? by Sheila Cole	Jan. 31, 1998
Quiet Strength by Rosa Parks & Gregory Reed	Feb 3, 1998
Malcolm X by Walter Dean Myers	late March
Black Like Me John Howard Griffin	early April
Hiroshima by John Hersey	April 1, 1998
To Kill a Mockingbird by Harper Lee	early April
Celine by Brock Cole	May 11, 1998
Shabanu by Suzanne Fisher Staples	

Name Nicole Haslan

An eighth grader's reading log, from September through May.

WHEN STUDENTS SELF-EVALUATE